Skill Stacking

A Practical Approach to Life, Beat the Competition and Do What You Love

By,

Steven West

Table of contents

Chapter one: Introduction

Chapter two: The Difference Between A Specialist and A Generalist and Why Being A Generalist is Better

Chapter three: Success Stories from Real People

Chapter four: Skill Stacking-What It Is and Why You Need to Learn How to Do It

Chapter five: Learning Styles

Chapter six: Meta Skills-What They Are and Why You Need Them

Chapter seven: Accelerated Learning Techniques

Chapter eight: Practice and Repetition

Chapter nine: Conclusion

Chapter one: Introduction

Many people enter the work force not realizing what it is that they want to be. This is fine as it happens to many people and in all honesty, for many people, it takes them years to figure it out. Some people think that being a generalist will serve their needs better, and others think that the right path to be taken is to become a specialist. There are many different approaches to this and ultimately the choice comes down to you. We will be taking the time to help you realize what a generalist is as well as what it is to be known as a specialist. There are merits and benefits to both, and we explain the difference between the two. There are also downsides to both, and we will be explaining those as well to give you the best information so that you, in turn, can make the best possible decision for yourself. Helping you realize the difference between the two is going to help you realize why one is better than the other and which one you will want to utilize for the most benefit in your life.

In the business world and in life there are certain skills that you will need to have and while being a specialist offers you many benefits being a generalist can offer you just as many benefits as well. It depends on what lifestyle you want to lead, and it depends on what it is you're trying to achieve for yourself. Many people, however, can agree that generalism is better than specialism in today's rapidly changing society because in many workplaces as the market and need for different skills change, a specialist may have more time finding work than a generalist. This is because a specialist is an expert at one thing while a generalist makes sure they are more flexible. Many companies like someone who is able to be more flexible. This is a book that will show you a detailed explanation of the differences between both while presenting facts as well as information to show you which can be more beneficial in the business world as well as life.

Another benefit that we will be discussing in this book is we will have actual examples of people who have made successful businesses or successful life careers from being generalists instead of specialists. One famous example is the actor Terry Crews. Another is Vice President Al Gore. We discuss both in this book to show how generalists and their skills benefitted them in their life and benefitted those around them. We also have examples of the concept of skills stacking which is another very important thing in the business world and the real world because it can offer you the ability to achieve a goal much more quickly. This is because you're combining separate skills to be successful. People also learn differently and as everyone is different, everyone has a different learning style and each of the different learning styles that have been known to our society today have very different benefits to help you become successful in your life and in your career. Meta skills are also something that we all need to succeed and almost every endeavor that you're going to encounter in your life will require you to have them. As such we will be discussing these skills as well so thar you will be able to see everything that you need to have a successful career or experience success in your life.

The celebrity examples that we have used in this book have been far reaching and we have made sure to include so many different people so that we can give you an idea of just how far being a generalist can go. What these people were interested in were completely different fields of expertise in completely different fields of the skills that they were using for themselves.

They made a difference in their lives and careers and they inspired other people to do the same by philanthropic efforts environmental efforts as well as showing people that you can do whatever you like with your passions and still be very successful while inspiring other people to do the same. By following their lead you can use these skills for yourself and make sure that you're able to make your own goals happen for yourself and to be able to make your success happen for yourself as well.

In anything that we do if you would like to get better the best thing that you can do it practice the art of repetition to learn it well and properly while your learning new skills. When we do this we learn quicker and it stays in our head because of the fact that were hearing it over and over. This is a very good skill for learning how to learn something much more quickly and to the point much more effectively. With the knowledge that you will be able to gain from this book you will be able to see that it is generalism and not specialism that is the way of the future instead of specialization and that it is a good idea to be to be great at many skills instead of just focusing on one skill because this will be able to help you further in life and in success.

This is why you should learn to be proficient in more than one skill. It's going to take you further in life because if you're skill set becomes obsolete like a specialist you have something else to fall back on. This also lets you be ahead of the curve. When the specialists are relearning what they have to, you will already know what you should be working on and what you need to know.

Others don't which is where you're going to be able to edge out your competition. Many people believe that this is the better option because in today's rapidly changing society technology is quickly edging out what skills you need. For the people who are still stuck in the past and only have one skill, they are losing work but for people who are embracing the future, they will be able to be the ones to find the work that they need to find and they will be the ones who are able to be more successful with it in the future. Companies are looking for innovative people that can wear a lot of hats because they can't afford to hire very many specialists as we will discuss in later chapters. So for many, it is a strong belief that a generalist would be of more use to their company than a specialist. With the knowledge in this book, you will be able to understand why this is a good book for you to understand this art for yourself and how it will be able to positively influence your life and career for the better.

Chapter two: The Difference Between A Specialist and A Generalist and Why Being A Generalist is Better

Many people think that being a specialist offers more benefit than being a generalist, but most people don't even know what those two terms mean. A generalist is a person who is proficient or competent in several different fields of study or several different fields of activity while a specialist is a person who concentrates mostly on a particular subject or mostly on a particular activity. This person would be highly skilled in a specific or restricted field meaning that they're an expert. The difference between a generalist and specialist is a generalist believes that if they are able to possess many skills it would be more useful. A specialist on the other hand usually tries to have detailed knowledge of a single study so that they can be considered a master or an expert in that particular field. In this chapter were going to take a look at both of these terms while exploring why being a generalist is better than being a specialist and why having many skills in different areas or being a Jack of all trade can be better for you than being a master at a single thing.

It is worth noting here that a specialist can have other skills beside that one, they just haven't mastered them. Likewise, a generalist has skills that they could master they simply decide that they would rather possess many skills. This is because they believe that possessing many skills will do them better. With that being said let's take a look at both and see why being a generalist is what most people think is better. In fields of technology and places like sales and human resources, it is said that specialists thrive, and they are the ones that get hired because they want to make sure that the person they hire knows what they are doing. In other words, they want the best. However, unfortunately for specialists, they can see their skills not being needed anymore in just a few short years. An example would be a travel agent. With the technology that is available to us when was the last time anyone needed a travel agent? Another example would be a photojournalist. Believe it or not, this field is actually dwindling because everyone thinks because they have a camera they can do the same job.

A generalist is more valued in smaller organizations. Smaller organizations typically cannot afford to hire very many specialists. This means that a generalist is what they need more for their companies. You will be valued in a small organization because they need their employees to wear a lot of hats. Many generalists can also be considered multipotentialities. Multipotentialities are people that have many exceptional talents but any one or more of those skills could make a great career for that person. An example would be gifted children. Gifted children have been considered by many to be multipotentialities. Their advanced abilities and their curiosity make them prime candidates for this term. Multipotentiality is a psychological and educational term that refers to the ability and the preference of a particular person. This person would be particularly one of artistic curiosity and strong intellect which in turn means that they excel in two or more different fields. This makes for an interesting cross between both the world of a generalist and a specialist.

Many people have different interests and they get bored with a job after a few years and they want to move on to something new. Others get new jobs every six months or less. These people are called job hoppers. They can't find a job that they find interesting, so they move from job to job and have many different skills. For some, this works for many it doesn't. Having this many jobs is not always beneficial however because it tells employers that you can be fickle and that you won't stay with them long. On the other hand, since many people may feel like they may need to keep things interesting and they need to change every year, the theory behind this happens to be that many people believe this is why becoming a generalist is better than being a specialist. They will be able to move between these companies much easier because they have more than one skill set so they can go between niches.

A specialist to someone who needs to stay on top of the areas that they are experts in and they're willing to move only when their skills become a commodity or obsolete. Being a specialist requires vigilance and the willingness to be able to move when the industry moves. You have to be aware that your industry could have destructive trends and that could mean the end of your job in certain cases. You have to be able to move when the industry moves because if you don't then they will find someone who will.

One of the problems with being a specialist is that when your skills are no longer needed they have trouble finding work because they haven't studied other things. A good example is to think about ten years ago, there were certain office skills that were needed, and everyone began to learn them so that they could find work. As the office world expanded the skills from ten years ago are the basics of what you need today which means those specialists have more to learn and their unprepared. Now that their skills have been rendered useless or at the very least obsolete, they need to learn new things which takes longer and could mean that they have difficulty finding work because they haven't learned other skills or become experts in other skills. This is another reason that most believe that generalism is better than specialism.

One of the most popular ideas in the business world and really in any aspect of our lives is that most people believe that successful people have achieved mastery. Many people believe that you have to master a skill to achieve career success. As a society were told to admire and glorify winners. We look at champions, billionaire's and gold medalists as winners and they are. They most certainly are. There are many lessons we can learn from people who are masters in a single particular skill but at the same time, not everyone has the ability to do that. This shouldn't make anyone feel bad as that's not a bad thing. Not everyone is made to master a single particular skill. In reality, not everybody wants to spend 20,000 hours or even 50,000 hours mastering a single skill. For the ones that do, and can that be great. Others, however, get bored and they feel their creative energy being wasted and sometimes some people can get depressed simply trying to learn that one skill instead of following their passions for many skills. Everyone has other things that they value in their life and that's not something to feel bad about either. Some people feel perfectly comfortable spending all that time learning those skills and others simply don't. This is another way the two are different from each other.

Here is some additional information about being a specialist and a generalist that you might find useful. It is said that you should be a specialist in your topic because the employer that you're talking to at the moment needs to know that you have a level of depth in that industry that is going to be competitive. Specialists can be more competitive in that area than generalists. You will have to research your prospective employees because you can't sell an employee on being a talented generalist who can learn. In many industries, no one wants to pay you to learn. They want to pay you for what you already know. This is another area and another one of the reasons that people consider a specialist to edge out a generalist.

A generalist is said to be great because they can be a generalist in their skills. When you want to understand the industry and you want to understand your role in it, you will want to put forward a breadth of skills that will get you hired. This is especially true if you're aiming for a job in management. In addition to having a specialty that's functional. For example, a direct response, digital technology, or skills of that nature would help you if you're working with marketing.

You also need to be able to relate to people which a generalist can do better in people's opinions. You can also manage people and budgets and other skills that are broader than your specific role. A specialist has more desire, and this is what an employer expects you to feel. They want you to know their business and they expect you to have a desire and a passion for the business. A generalist can have passion, but you should want to have a passion like that specialist. You don't want to put all of your eggs in one basket, which is something that specialists have a problem with. This is because they've exhausted all of their time and effort into becoming a master at a single skill. The employer is going to be looking at other candidates that have more than one skill though there are those that prefer a specialist for their dedication. If they want a generalist you need to make them feel like their choice is your first choice. You need to show them that you have the passion and the courage to work for their company and you need to make them believe that their company and their industry is the right choice for you. This is what's going to get you hired over people that aren't going to get hired. They want to believe that you really want this job and they want you to show them your passion for what you're making them believe about you. This is going to edge you out over your competition.

A generalist's ability to have a broad range of issues would be able to see deeper inside and be able to see the interconnectedness and find solutions that a specialist might not be able to see because they're so focused on other things. All the different departments within a job and in business let's say, would connect with each other because all the jobs in a business and the different department within a business all connect to each other. A generalist might be able to be able to see the bigger picture and they would be more likely to come up with different ideas and different solutions that would benefit the entire business not just part of it.

Most people don't view the world through a single lens. Instead, they have a broader approach and a broader understanding of different things which can help make them be able to make better decisions. This is why a generalist can see the big picture and they are considered to be able to think outside the box. They also tend to have more transferable skills and with the workplace changing rapidly transferable skills are becoming more and more important.

Businesses are constantly taught about scalability and its importance. It's important and essential for the workforce and they come in handy in many situations which is why we said that a generalist should wear a lot of hats. Generalists are usually managers and leaders in organizations, and this comes down to the skills that we just mentioned. If you don't know how to manage employees then you won't be able to do it but if you do know how to manage employees then you'll be able to do this no matter what business that you're in or whatever industry that you're in. It wouldn't be of much importance to the industry. The skills that you possess would be important. The disadvantage of being a generalist would be that they are sacrificing depth for the chance to have breadth. The increased complexity would also make it harder to have that in depth

understanding of things and that is why
generalists are considered only to be
looking at the surface of things. Think of
an iceberg. A generalist would be able to
see the iceberg and it would be able to
analyze the ship's course and analyze the
icebergs importance to that course, but
the generalists couldn't have a deeper
knowledge of the iceberg and could be
missing vital information on what's
happening below the surface of the
iceberg. Generalists also have loosely
defined roles and they work in a number
of different areas as well as different
positions which means that they might
not have job security. If they do it might
suffer. It's very easy to replace one
generalist with another generalist.

Other advantages to be a specialist are
that a specialist has a career route that
has the ability and the chance to earn
them more money because they are an
expert in what they do. Companies are
willing to pay more for experts because
they understand that what they're
paying is for quality. When you were
hiring someone you want the person
who knows what they're doing not the

person who needs to be trained extra and needs time to get to where the other person already is. This is where a specialist can be better than a generalist.

A specialist has gained knowledge of whatever particular subject they're experts in. This means that since their positions are narrowly defined in a way that generalists aren't, the salaries tend to be much higher even when they're just starting out. The organizations have often found that specialists operating in different sectors are useful because that means organizations, on the whole, can rely on their expertise.

This is why the position of a specialist could be of extreme value for a company. They also provide the specialist with more internal power that a generalist wouldn't have. The reason that the generalist wouldn't have that kind of power yet is that they haven't gotten that high up on the ladder.

A specialist might be better placed to negotiate deals or negotiate when it comes to having a say in making new management structures or other issues of that nature. A specialist has the opportunity to become a true thought leader in that area of expertise if they are passionate about the subject and if they are willing to take their studies even further they could become a widely recognized leader in whatever field they are an expert in. The ability to become a leader of such stature can further improve your career prospects as well and open you up to much more opportunities in the field that you have chosen. People tend to seek experts rather than generalists when they are actually encountered with a problem but a disadvantage of being a specialist is that a single subject can have its drawbacks. A generalist has a wide range of career options, but specialist don't because they have a narrow field in expert skills which means they can only find work in that one field. Available job opportunities become smaller when you compare them to the generalist. For that reason, you can learn more in your expertise later just as you could go from being a generalist to a specialist if that's what you choose to do. You are also more likely to be the go to expert in your field of work because you're the expert. Your opinion and input are probably the most appreciated if the topic at hand involves your field directly.

Even though they had better earning opportunities, finding suitable positions may be tougher because of that narrow field that we've already mentioned and in some cases there are plenty of specialists competing for the same position because of that narrow field. This means that if you do decide to become a specialist then you'd have to stand out from the crowd. However, in this chapter, we have given you vital information and shown that most companies though not all, do prefer the benefits of having a generalist on their payroll and not a specialist because a generalist has more skills to offer than that specialist. Another reason is the company would be able to afford a generalist better than a specialist as well.

Chapter three: Success Stories from Real People

When we think about being a generalist it might be hard to come up with one that we actually feel like we know in our personal lives. However, there are many celebrities that are actually generalists and have turned it into a very successful career. Many celebrities are lucky to only have one household appliance to their name such as George Foreman and his grill. This isn't a bad thing though. It's a good thing that turned into a profitable business and helped him get his goal achieved. Other celebrities however have their hands in everything from perfume to books which shows that being a generalist is something that can really pay off in the business world.

If you think about someone like Steve Jobs for example. He has created many different electronics that you can use for your pocket and your car or wherever you need to go. You have the iPad, a smart phone or iPod and laptops that you can take everywhere in your daily life to stay connected. He is creating relevant and functional products for people to use and it's because he has remained personally involved and personally invested in each and every one. He could have specialized in business and become a CEO. This is something that he was able to achieve for himself, but he could have specialized on just being a CEO instead he was constantly learning and caring about what people wanted and trying to give it to them. He understands the importance of what people need. One thing that sets him apart from others is that he even answers his own email which a lot of celebrities don't do anymore but as he thinks it's important he does. It's this type of thing that sets him apart from other people who are specialists.

Another example is Al Gore. Al Gore could have limited himself to specializing in politics, but he never did. He was known for being the vice president of the United States. An important thing to note however is that he didn't want to be just a footnote in a history book, instead he wanted to go further. Because he did now he's a respected author as well as being dedicated to the environment.

Now everyone knows him as a dedicated environmentalist who's trying to make the world better and he has received a Nobel peace prize. For many generalists their path could emerge later on in life, but the key point is the same. The work that Al Gore was able to do for the environment was able to inspire hundreds of thousands of people to begin to understand that they wanted to help the environment as well. Because of this, there have been plans put into place to try and make the world a better place and to help stop environmental issues that most people didn't care about before he said anything or made his movie. Because he has however people now see that the environment needs help and that we should be doing something to help.

A broad knowledge base and having versatile skills can bring you many opportunities in your life. Martha Stewart is another great example from her early career from being a model to be a stockbroker and then afterwards a caterer. Martha Stewart has followed her passions over the years to become a great entrepreneur. She does everything from weddings, to kitchen basics, kids crafting, and holiday ideas. If Martha Stewart had decided to specialize in one thing it would still have a success but instead she decided to follow her passions and be a generalist. Now she is known as the ultimate entrepreneur and many look up to her. Martha Stewart is recognized as one of the best cooks, decorators and crafters of an entire generation and she's been able to inspire people to find their creative passions through her website and her books. She's even been able to inspire people to come out and find their creative passions as well.

Richard Branson is another great example of how being a generalist can be a great avenue for your career. His company Branson's Virgin Group is in the center of over 400 different enterprises. They do everything from beverages to airlines. They are also in the center of cell phones and comic books, online gaming, hotels and even green technology and healthcare. That's just his business life. He is known for being an adventurer and a very well-known public figure as well as being an amazing philanthropist in his life as well. He never put limits on himself and even though he dropped out of school at age 16 he has managed to make an entire career out of himself for being a generalist. He believes that opportunities are like busses and there's always another one coming. This is a very famous quote that he's been known for saying and he's another great example of how generalism is better than specialism.

Richard Branson is a great example about how having your company and having it be in many different things can be a great thing for generalists because he was able to put his company in the center of so many other different genres that he was able to achieve worldwide success and he's able to indulge himself in his passions and his hobbies while inspiring others. He had been covered in

YouTube videos, television and many other venues so that he was able to get his business and passions recognized.

If you need another example of an amazing great female who is a general list instead of a specialist. We have one. Think of Oprah. Everyone in the world has heard of Oprah and she's famous in the United States as well as other countries for her wonderful work that she does. She doesn't have a political science degree, but she was still able to help the president. In 2008 Obama was running for president and she was able help him seal the election.

She's not a teacher but she was able to find successful schools and didn't let the lack of a teaching degree stop her. The same was true with writing. She wasn't a writer, but she has managed to succeed with one of the most successful magazines in the United States. To her credit she is not a licensed therapist but that didn't matter at all to the millions of people who have been touched by her talk show over the years and who were touched by the wonderful love that she showed all of her fans and then the rest of the world that she was trying to help. Oprah has been an amazing woman and she's inspired many women and men across the globe with her show, her books and how she's able to inspire people to do better and be the best versions of themselves. Being a generalist helps her find her passion in many different fields and she's been able to utilize that to not only make her life better but make other people's lives better as well.

Terry Crews is another great example of being a generalist. He is known for being an activist and an artist. A former American football player and comedian as well as an actor. When he first started his career, he was a linebacker in the NFL for the Rams, the Redskins and then the Chargers. He was also in the World League of American Football with Reign Fire and he was a college football player at the University of Western Michigan. However he was smart enough to know that you can play sports forever as you can't do anything forever and he was able to use his other skills to his advantage and become one of the most celebrated actors in Hollywood known for his kind and friendly manner and easy going nature. This has made people follow him and want to buy whatever he is endorsing. It's also made him more successful because he has a good attitude and it shows.

Had he just stayed with football he still would have been famous, but he wouldn't be the person that we know today. The person that we know today has become a jack of all trades and he's not only a football player but now he is an advocate for women's rights. He is also an activist against sexism. He has recently gone public with stories of sexual assault to help other victims of this horrible affliction. He has also had an amazing acting career since 1997 when he left the football world. He has played mainly comedic roles, but he has starred in action films as well.

His illustration and portraiture are well loved in the art world and he's even the co-founder of a design company called Amen&Amen. If he had just stuck with one thing he would never been able to achieve all of this but because he decided to be a generalist he was able to achieve much more in his career and open himself to new possibilities.

Tim Ferriss is another example of why it's better to be a generalist than specialist. He grew up in New York and graduated from school before receiving a degree in East Asian studies from Princeton. After he graduated he started to work in a data status storage company doing sales, but he began his own internet business while still employed with that company. After he founded his own company he sold it to a private equity firm and began to write books. He is now celebrated as a successful author. He is also an angel investor and advisor and makes podcasts and television shows. This is not only a great thing to do as an entrepreneur but it's a great way to get yourself noticed by your fans and the people that your trying to reach. These days he's described as a self-help guru and known to help many people using his wonderful talents and he's able to reach many people with his words.

Britney Spears is another wonderful example. Many singers have decided to open their own clothing lines, perfumes, and television and Britney has done the same. Britney Spears is a famous singer and she is also considered to be a generalist because that's not the only thing she stayed in. She is an amazing singer, and this is where she stayed and made most of her money, but she branched out and she released a multi-platinum video game. She has received a lot of fans and gained popularity for her Pepsi commercials as well. Over the years she has announced a new clothing line and a new clothing brand and along with that she's designed limited edition lines for her brands. To branch out in music she's released music videos with different companies to branch out into a new avenue and she's teamed up with games like Twister Dance as well.

One of the things that she received many new fans for is she has designed her own perfume scents she designed her first perfume in the early 2000s and she has designed seven more in rapid succession. Not too long after that she went on to design even more in a later year.

Since then she has sold over one million bottles of her perfumes and was able to sell even more through clever product placement by having her perfumes in her videos. One in particular was massively and widely popular and it shot her perfume sales through the roof. After she accomplished this she even created her own role playing game in 2016. As early as last year she announced her twelfth fragrance and last year she had released twenty four fragrances through Elizabeth Arden. Like others on this list she is a philanthropist and she has established the Britney Spears Foundation which is a charitable entity that helps children in need. She has sung along with other artists for their Artists Against Aids Worldwide and she's raised money for other projects as well as donating money to cancer foundation's. She is a very good example of how branching out and being interested in many different things can help you become successful and can help you go further in your career. If she had just stuck with singing she still would have been just as famous as she is now because she has made over

5 million dollar albums. Because she branched out in philanthropic endeavors and has made her own perfume and clothing lines people got to see an entirely new different side to her. When this happened they began to like her in a completely new way.

Faith Hill is a country music singer who has been a very famous generalist as well. Many people know her because of her faith as a Christian and the fact that she appeared on television and many other people know her because she starred in films as well as being an internationally known country music star. She's also expanded her interests into perfume and philanthropy however which brought more success. She has supported national children's book drives and has her own literacy project where her fans were able to donate books at a concert and they were actually able to get over 30,000 children's books that were distributed into libraries, schools and hospitals. In addition to this she has also joined in efforts to take supplies to Mississippi after it was hit by hurricane Katrina and her husband and herself have hosted several charity concerts for people in need and raised money for other foundations as well. As a country singer she has found lots of love in the industry of singing and obviously that is one of the main things that makes her happy. However it's good for us to see that she was able to become a generalist and use the other skills that she has at her disposal to make other things happen for herself. Now she is known as a well-known actress, philanthropist and fragrance owner. Her perfumes have been very popular, and she has other business ventures that she has been looking into as well.

Tyler Perry is most famous for his hilarious characters and his movies but also the fact that he is a Christian man that is putting good Christian movies out there for people to watch and learn a life lesson during each of his movies. However, he is a partner with celebrities like Oprah for television shows and he has made his own studios for his movies. He has written books and been on stage. All of these pursuits that

he has done have made him wildly
famous and incredibly successful in his
life and it has been shown that he has
been able to pursue his passions in other
areas as well.

Mary Kay and Ashley Olsen have been in
the industry of acting since they were
still in diapers. When they were very
young and still in their baby years, they
were on television and they are known
for being on television by fans across the
United States. By the time they were
teenagers they had made over 25 movies
together. As early as the 2000s, they
continued to be releasing movie after
movie in rapid succession. After that
they started appearing on television
instead of making movies and they had
their own sitcom as well. They were able
to receive a daytime Emmy Award and
they had their own fan club as well. The
fan club had items such having photos
and collectibles of each person and they
had T shirts posters, key rings and other
items. They were very popular in the
preteen market during the late 1990s
and 2000s.

Because of this their names and likenesses were in movies and videos across the globe. Along with that they had books, purses, shoes, clothing, and make up before they extended their talents into board games and video games, calendars and even telephones and CD players. The company Mattel even produced various sets of fashion dolls from the years 2000 to 2005 in their likeness, along with separate outfits and accessory packs. They became copresidents of Dualstar when they turned 18 and they made moves to secure the future of the company by releasing products that appealed to teen markets and the tween market. This included fragrances and home decoration.

Once they became a little older they also started a career in fashion and their own clothing line. They signed and made pledges allowing full maternity leave to all workers that sewed for their lines of clothing and as such the National Labor Committee that had organized the pledge in the first place, praised the twins and their commitment to worker rights. After that they then launched another fashion label for couture in London and then a contemporary collection which was inspired by unique finds and pieces in their personal wardrobes.

They've released a clothing line for JC Penney, and they published a book in 2008. When 2013 hit they decided to launch another fashion line and began racking up awards as early as 2012 through 2015. They are the perfect example of how being a generalist can help you become world famous and they've been acting since they were around 9 months old and were steady in work from 1987 to 2004 just in movies and television shows. As soon as the television shows and the movies stopped and they became more interested in fashion, they've opened many fashion lines and clothing lines before taking up being authors for a bestselling book. They have branched out into many different avenues and made then successfully work as well as having many different interests. This can help you and it can bring you many accolades of success.

Teens everywhere around the world have heard of Justin Bieber. He made an entire generation of teens fall in love with him and skyrocketed to fame after being noticed on YouTube. Not only as he is singer, but he is also used his talents and his reputation for his own generalist purposes. He has different passions and skills that he likes to use to his benefit, and he's invested in businesses from all over including Spotify, sojo and tiny chat. Over the years he's also come out with many different items that have been available in stores to sell such as headphones and other marketable items.

The Kardashian's are another one of the most famous families known in the United States and they have their hands in just about everything. They've made movies they've made music. Along with that they have their own television show series and they've been able to join the fashion industry, the makeup industry and many more industries as well. They've managed to inspire millions of women and men across the United States and other countries as well and they've shown that being a generalist can make you millions of dollars as long as you have the right attitude and motivation and the determination to make it happen for yourself.

The Rock has been one of the most influential actors especially in recent years, but he didn't start out that way. Originally he started out as a football player and then later a wrestler. After he had a football career that was successful. He moved on to be a professional wrestler and did an amazing job and quickly rose to the ranks of fame. He broke many different records and was well known for his persona and what he stood for as a wrestler as well as his catch phrase. However, he has also appeared on television and he's appeared in many different films. He has appeared in magazines and expanded his horizons into being an author that was on the best seller list for several weeks.

He even founded his own production company and he has also produced his own reality competition series. He has partnered with the fitness apparel Under Armor. Through Under Armor he has released several different apparel items that have sold out fairly quickly every time they're released. For example, when he first partnered with them and had a gym bag, it sold out in just a couple of days. Understanding the need for social media he also has a YouTube channel that is named after himself and has help from an online personality that's on YouTube as well.

It was because he was able to follow his passions and understand that being a generalist was better than being a specialist that he was able to make a massively successful career for himself and he was able to inspire other people around the world with his films, his career and his social media presence.

He has also made a very big difference with his activism and philanthropy. He attended democratic national conventions and inspired people to vote and explained why it was so important. He also had a speaking role at a different convention that same year. He has founded his own charity foundation which is designed to help terminally ill children and he donates large amounts of money to athletic departments and foundations that help students. The University of Miami actually renamed their locker room after him in his honor.

He has also donated to GoFundMe to pay for abandoned dogs' surgeries and he's donated to hurricane Harvey. His help didn't stop there, however. He has donated to military bases and after Hawaii was flooded he worked with nonprofit organizations to help repair damages caused by those floods. He's even worked with Make A Wish foundation on a number of occasions. This was cause for him to gain an entirely new fan base that respected him for the fact that he was trying to help the planet and the people in it with his heart and his influence.

Alfonso Ribeiro is most known for being an American Actor on the Fresh Prince of Bel-Air. What people don't know is that he is not just an actor. He is a comedian, a dancer, a director and a television personality. He is a generalist in every sense of the word, and he is able to use his passions in every aspect of his life as well as being able to use it for his success. He was able to star in steady work and over the years as had job after job in rapid succession and hasn't stopped. He has been able to take over for other hosts in the television world and make sure that he is still recognizable in today's society and has avoided the traps that most celebrities fall into. Because of that fact he is consistent with his work and doesn't have to worry about his skills not being needed. He is a professional through and through and because of his attitude toward people they respect him, and they keep offering him work as a result.

He has directed and found passion as a singer and a dancer. He has found success in both areas and he was even able to compete on Dancing with the Stars and came in 4th. He has been able to stay famous and stay relevant through his ability to understand that a being a generalist is better than being a specialist and has used his dancing skills to make sure that no matter how many years have passed he will always be recognizable and never forgotten. He didn't just stick to acting but he stuck of his passions instead and was able to do other things as well. Through his work he has gained a very large and loyal fan base and many people look up to his career as a mark of success.

Chuck Norris is wildly popular among martial artists and fans of the martial arts world. Many people have seen his movies and many people know that he is very much a generalist. If you didn't know very much about Chuck Norris many would say that he was a specialist because you would only think he was in martial arts and acting. However people that really know his career and have followed him over the years understand that he is a generalist because he is a screen writer along with being an actor.

Martial arts of course were his main passion but along with being a martial artist and a film producer, he served in the United States Air Force. Then he tried his hand at writing books. Over the years he has written several books on everything from the Christian faith, to a biography, philosophy, politics, exercise and Western novels.

His novels have made the best times selling list twice and he has been a steady influence on many people and their lives with many teenagers quoting him and looking up to him.

He is another philanthropist and he has established a Fighting Arts Federation and Kickstart Kids. He helps at risk children and tries to keep them away from drug related pressure by helping them train in martial arts. To help the planet, he has his own ranch where they bottle water and a portion of each, and every sale supports environmental funds.

His foundation that he has made for children has made fans look up to him for his kindness and he is also known for contributing toward organizations for children, veterans, hospitalized veterans and he has also worked with the Make A Wish Foundation.

He served as a spokesperson with the United States Veterans Administration and he has made the issues that have concerned people about hospitalized war veterans and made people aware of pension and health care issues. Due to his continued support he has received the Veteran of the Year Award. He was also gifted the American Veteran's Award.

Taking his philanthropy even further he supported Indian foundations which brought hope, help and healing to defenseless and innocent victims of tragedy, disease in circumstance and tried to help make the situation better. He has also donated money to help aids and a blind school overseas as well as helping missions. In his professional career he expanded his horizons even further when he made video games over the years. He is an amazing example of how a generalist can have very different skills and passions and how to use them all to help people and inspire people as well as being coming wildly successful and inspiring other people to do the same.

Many of these celebrities have shown that you can follow your passions and make a difference in this world. Many of them could have stayed in their field that they were in and they would have been just as famous as if they hadn't followed their passions for other avenues, but they didn't do that the choose to follow their passions and they chose to branch out a little and make themselves happy. They chose this instead of being a specialist in one field. They wanted the freedom to explore multiple avenues and many different fields to get involved in. As such we have some innovative inventions that have come from their imagination and creativity. We have read inspiring books and were able to see the shape that the world is in just based on some of the examples that we've used in this book. They have also had many different innovative ideas for fashion and other industries as well. If the celebrities had not branched out we wouldn't have any of that because they wouldn't have done it. You can follow their lead and find out what your passions are and what your skill sets are and learn what it is that you want to do as a generalist. You might find that you are a good writer and that you want to write a book, or you might find that you like volunteering and donating money for philanthropy causes. Which is a noble goal that many celebrities have had over the years. Many of the celebrities have given millions of dollars to many charities and even raised money for awareness of different causes all over the globe. Another thing you could find that you like is making money and selling things. This could be where another skill set lies. Everyone has different skills and different things that make them unique and special, but you can see from these examples that we've been able to show you that real people who started out just as normal people were able to use their skills to make themselves massively successful. If they are making it there's no reason why you shouldn't be able to do it for yourself as well.

Chapter four: Skill Stacking-What It Is and Why You Need to Learn How to Do It

Skills stacking is another very important part of becoming a generalist but it's also important to becoming more successful in your life. Skill stacking is a beautiful skill set that will not only translate into your business life, but it will translate into her personal life as well. Many companies that are hiring people these days prefer generalists that have many skills that they are good at or they prefer people that are generalists that are able to learn several different skills. The art of skill stacking is very useful in this avenue and in this chapter we are going to it explain to you what skill stacking is and how to use it for your benefit.

Skill stacking is the concept of skill stacking is the ability or the desire to learn specific skills to achieve a goal and then combining those skills to be successful. Sometimes pursuing opportunities to gain a deeper level of experience with a skill you already have is really beneficial. Other times you should pursue opportunities that can give you a wider skill set, or a broader skill set. Skill stacking is learning new skills and combining them to do unique new things that are going to help you. For each new skill that you can add to your agenda you could gain multiple new skills that you didn't have before. So for example if you have figured out new skills for yourself and then you add a new skill on top of that for yourself, you might have more than 3 total skills now. The reason for this being is that that new skill could also have something to do with an existing skill which is going to create another skill. This is called skill stacking and how it comes to be.

A really good example for you will be to imagine yourself in a video game character and that you're starting off at the beginning. So in the beginning you only have 2 skills you can punch and jump but that's all you're allowed to do. Now this is great for when things are coming at you because you can jump over them or you can punch through them. Since that's all you can do, you can't really do much more than that. For the moment you have two ways to avoid objects.

When you learn to crouch, you have added a new skill. Now you have two ways of avoiding attacks and one way of fighting them. Now say you learn how to run. You're now good for three skills. You don't have to wait for things to come to you now you can go to them and you can walk and move around in addition to what you could do already. You can use your new skill of running with your previous skills of punching and being able to crouch and jump. All of these skills work well together, and you've gone from having just the basic skills. You have four skills but since you can also use this skill with your other skills technically you now have 7 skills because you can run and punch, you can run and jump, or you can run and crouch. This means that you've added 3 skills by only having a single new skill. This is where the art of skill stacking comes in.

Skill stacking is being able to add more and more skills to the ones you already have. In this situation you've only added a single new skill, but you got 3 skills from that one skill. An important thing to remember is that this doesn't happen every time. In many cases a single new skill is just a single new skill. The ones you add and the ones you gained by combining skills can be valuable in their own rights. You should also know that the more valuable skills that you have, the more opportunities you are going to be able to use and the more opportunities you are going to be able to get.

This is where you begin to start earning things and to help your career. If you need a real world example instead of a video game we can do that too. You work in an office and you're on a team. You are good with excel. You learn that if you're good with excel, then you're comfortable with data manipulation and you can create graphs and simple charts. From there you can see that your good at power point that's nothing fancy but you're learning how to put bullets in your presentations, adding graphics and text. You have now added another skill to your arsenal and now you have 2 skills. Because of these 2 skills you have access to a 3rd skill which is reporting. This is because you can create the graphs and the charts in Excel and then you can put them in PowerPoint. This means you can create useful reports for your team or your management. Now your company knows that you have a new skill. As do you.

You can also stack the skills that you learn outside of work and watch these pay off in your career as well. Many people love reading books and the opportunity to learn new subjects. You could also have a hobby like being able to talk to people that can be useful at work. Say for example that you like to make videos for YouTube or maybe you would like to build things on the weekend. Your company can then take that as a sign that you would be good at marketing because you have video skills and editing skills or if you like to build things, they might let you try and build a new prototype for your company because you have skills in that area as well in your life. You should look for new skills that you can stack, and you should do this for your career as well. That way when you're ready you can have new and valuable opportunities that can open up for you at work and you will be prepared for them. These opportunities will not only increase your earnings but also add variety to your career.

You don't need to become the best person in the world to be successful. All you need is skill sets that you can use to achieve career success. Many people first get a job when they're 17 or 18 and still young. Most people go to college after that and are only slightly older if they decide to wait. Even if you don't go to college you still have valuable skill sets that you can use for people and that you can use for your career. Many people have skills with public speaking skills as well as having persuasion skills and many people understand the importance of being on time.

So they have skills to begin with already. Another thing you should know is that every skill you have doubles your odds of success. Think about it like this. How many people around you, do you know who are not the best in the world at anything and they're still doing well in their career? It's not about being perfect. It's about increasing your odds. You'll have a better shot of having a good career if you have more skills. If you're a one trick pony your options are very limited and remember if those skills are not needed anymore then you're going to have to learn new ones anyway.

If you have multiple skills that you're good at then you're more valuable and that's what career success is going to ultimately be about. The skills that you should be able to have and the skills that you should be able to stack are all around you. If you are able to utilize these skills for yourself they can stack into hundreds of other skills. In particular there are 5 skills that you can really use and by unlocking these 5 alone, you'll be able to stack hundreds of other skills.

The 5 skills that you need to utilize for yourself to unlock hundreds of other skills is productivity, personal finance, persuasion, psychology and writing. There's a reason that productivity is first on the list. You need to be a person who can get stuff done. If you're a person who can get things done you will always find a way to get those things done. If you have solid productivity skills you'll be able to learn anything for yourself. This is why this is the first one on the list. This is because you need to understand the importance of time and you need to understand the importance of getting things done. If you are someone who is not able to get things done no company will want to work with you.

The second skill that you need is psychology. Psychology is a basic understanding of people and yourself. You need to be able to understand why it is you do what you do and why other people do what they do. This doesn't mean you have to go to school to become a psychologist and it doesn't mean you have to read 100 books on psychology either. All that it means is that you need to understand the basics so that you'll be able to understand people better and understand yourself better. A very important tool in business and in your career as well as in your personal life is to understand why people are how they are and why they do what they do because this will help you do better in the business world.

Writing is another important business tool that you're going to need to understand how to do because it's the ability to translate your thoughts into words and this makes it easier for people to do their jobs. When you're able to write in a way that is simple and clear you can express yourself in a new way and very few people are able to express themselves this way. This puts you ahead of the pack.

The art of persuasion is one of the most important things you can learn for the business world because being able to understand persuasion will ensure that you're better at holding conversations, public speaking, sales and leadership. Anything that requires influencing others you will be able to do with this skill. If you're able to persuade people effectively then you're able to unlock hundreds of skills with this. Influencing people is more about effective communication than anything else and in the business world effective communication is vital.

The last skill is personal finance and this one doesn't get mentioned a lot. Not nearly as much as it should. We don't often think about managing our money when we're young but when we get closer to retirement we might panic. We may think 'why didn't I start saving earlier' or 'why wasn't I smart earlier'? The time to start managing your personal finances is now. If you are able to unlock these skills and acquire these skills as well, it's going to turn you into a reliable human being that a company would want to hire. It also turns you into someone that people will want to be around. Another great benefit is that you'll be able to lock unlock hundreds of other skills for yourself and stack those skills for your personal life and your career.

If you acquire these skills it will turn you into a reliable human being who's a generalist and who has many skills that a company would want, and a company would need. A question that you need to ask yourself is the following. If you were a business owner would you want to hire somebody who is only good at one thing, or the person who has the potential to unlock hundreds of different things?

Chapter five: Learning Styles

Everyone is different and because of this everyone has different learning styles. Some people are really easy to teach, and some people are harder to teach. Some people are able to pick up on things right away and for other people it takes longer simply because their learning style isn't being recognized or because they learn a different way. When people learn in different ways sometimes it isn't recognized by businesses or schools which makes things harder. Thankfully businesses are learning and adapting everyday so that their workers are understood better and they are able to be more helpful to their companies because of this.

There are 4 major types of learners and this chapter is going to explain what they are and how you can use them to further your goals and success in a professional environment as well as your personal life when you are trying to better yourself and understand yourself better. We give examples of how these types of learning are best for some people and we give examples of what these types of learnings look like. The 4 types of learners that you will need to be aware of for this chapter and learn about are the following.

1. The visual learner. This is a learner that learns best by seeing.
2. The auditory learner. This is a learner that learns best by hearing and sound.
3. The kinesthetic learner. This is a learner that is able to learn the best by doing things.
4. The reading and writing learner. This learner is able to learn the best when they are able to read and write.

Visual learner:

The first type of learner that we have is the visual learner. The visual learner is a learner that is able to see information and then visualize the relationships and ideas that are being shown to them. This is a very common learner and most people are able to identify with them easily as they learn the same way. Visual learners obviously work well and much better when they are in an environment where they can see what they need to know. This of course makes sense because it's right there in the title. Visual.

Because they work better by seeing you need to give them something to look at. Visual learners are able to work really well when you give them graphics or charts and they have a great ability to make presentations more visible for you when they get the opportunity. It is said that in this area, they may thrive though it's important to remember that even within these four aspects of learning people still learn differently and at different paces so that is something that is important to remember in this aspect.

Another benefit to visual learners is that they are able to make a presentation more visual to others to help them see the information being presented clearly and concisely to make sure that others don't have a problem with making the presentation work. Even for those that are not visual learners it is a big help when you are able to see the information clearly and without any issues at hand.

These types of learners are also able to showcase their skills in another beneficial way as well. visual learners able to show really good relationships between the various points of information. This is a very useful skill that many like to have in their arsenal. Because of this skill that they process this makes them a very valuable person to have on a team. They can help with presentations and other aspects of the business world that a company is going to be able to use. In every business there is a need for one of the learners on this list and ideally many say that a company needs all 4 because it would offer additional benefits.

Some additional advantages of visual learning are that it makes communication quicker and it makes communication a lot more simple. All of the information that is transmitted to the brain in a day or in your lifetime are 90% visual. That's a lot of information and in fact that's a huge percentage. Visuals are also processed 60,000 times faster than text, so when you're reading text it's obviously visual but seeing a visual is going to be processed faster.

40% of the nerve fibers are linked to the retina and the human eye can register over 30,000 visual messages in a single hour. Another thing you might now be aware of is that our brain can see images only for 13 milliseconds. That's how long they last. Humans are capable of getting a feeling or a sense of a visual scene in 1/10 of a second or less as well. As such all of these reasons are reasons that visuals are better for these people that will learn visually, and you also get to help store the information longer. Remember also that images are the most effective way to make sure that the information that you're wanting to learn is getting stored in your long term memory. Your short term memory can only process about 7 bits of information at once and it can only process words. however, your long term memory is able to process images and they can stay there in your long term memory.

It is also better for comprehension because visual learners can grasp concepts more easily by stimulating their imagination and affecting their cognitive capabilities that their brain has as well. Another benefit is that visual language is known to be able to stretch our bandwidth. What this means is that we are comprehending, analyzing and trying to understand and absorb new information. It drives motivation because visual learners have captivating images that we want to see or interesting graphics. They also want to be able to see engaging videos as learning aids because that helps visual learners fight boredom and it helps motivate them to do better.

It also is able to stimulate your emotions because visual stimulate and emotional response are linked, and it is together that these two will generate memories. Unsuitable visuals equal unhappy learners because as visuals are so important to this learning style we want to see something engaging and we want to see something that is going to cause an emotion in us.

So if the images are unappealing or unsuitable that's going to effect the visual learners because they won't be engaged in the meeting or the job. They are going to get bored or they will tune themselves out even if they don't mean to do so. What this means for these learners is that their power boosters are going to be their visuals.

A visual learner is such an asset because once they see something, they're able to understand it much better and they're able to put that knowledge and ability to good use. This is turn is going to offer great benefits to any company that they are wanting to work for in the first place.

Auditory learner:

The second type of learner that we have on this list is what is known as an auditory learner. Auditory means sound or hearing and anything that is related to the two. This means that an auditory learner is going to be someone who prefers to hear the information rather than reading it or rather than seeing it put in front of them on a chart. Hearing the information lets them absorb it and retain it because that's the way that works best for them. Seeing charts or graphs won't help them in the same way that it would help the visual learners because the two learn differently. You would need to try a different approach here so that they would be able to understand the information for themselves.

So they differ from visual learners because instead of seeing if they need to hear it. Auditory learners have a preference for reciting information out loud because it offers them the benefit of being able to hear the sounds and information as it's being told to them or them telling themselves. They can hear each piece of information as it is being said and this is what is going to be able to help them learn the information much more effectively and much more quickly. This also offers benefits to their company because they are good at focusing when people are talking.

An auditory leaner needs to say the information to themselves over and over however, because they need to hear it over and over to remember the information in some cases this can take a little time. Some only need to hear it once and these are very good auditory learners because they have an advantage over the ones that need to repeat it over and over again. Either way that your able to do this for yourself is good. If this is you than this is still a good way of learning and no one needs to feel that if they're not able to learn the same way as another person or if they're not able to learn as quickly that it's a bad thing because it's not.

Everyone in this world has different preferences and everyone's brain is wired differently. Some have issues with their mind that can affect the way they learn, and other's learn at different rates which means that different things work for different people. Companies know this and in your career you will find that while many aren't understanding, there are just as many that are. For an auditory learner what you should do is give them a chance to repeat everything back to you and repeat your points back to you as well. They can hear the information this way and let it sink into their mind so they can remember the information for when they will need it later.

One thing that you should do for them to make sure that they are learning at the best of their ability is to make sure that you ask them questions and then call upon them for answers. This lets them hear the information, but it shows the company or whoever that they are working for, that they have retained the information and can repeat it back to you to let you know that they've gotten what you're trying to say. An example to make this clearer and easier to understand is to think of going to meet your favorite author or actor. Or if you go to a panel. There is a question and answer session where information is passed back and forth and your able to learn what you need to, but it sticks in your head.

It is able to stick in your head because you're hearing the words that they are saying to you back and forth. Hearing it is what is able to infiltrate your brain. Another thing that this is like is think of a song that you hear on the radio. We have said that auditory learners hear something over and over and remember it right? You hear a song over and over and you remember it as well. This goes hand in hand with the practice and repetition that we will be discussing in a later chapter. Repetition would help this type of learner because they can hear the words repeatedly.

Other benefits of auditory learning are that the learners themselves are said to have increased retention which we've already discussed a little bit. But people who abdicate for this type of learning also say that because they're good listeners they have the ability to process information better than others and that they're able to retain it better because of it. Audio recordings are helpful with these learners as well because it increases the possibility of improved retention in your memory bank.

We've already discussed that people don't really believe in multitasking, but some do, and we've also discussed that there's more research that needs to be done about this, but one advantage of auditory learning is that people believe that it allows people to multitask because they can just listen to an audio recording. Because of that they can still have free hands and they can do other things as well as absorbing the information that they are needing.

There are many sources online available in the market or on the internet for people to get information. You can also get information from podcasts and other audio recording materials which means that there's a lot of availability for learning this way, but there's something to take note of. Just like there's advantages to learning this way, there are also disadvantages because there's chances of you being prone to distractions. This is because if you're in a classroom and you're listening to an audio recording, the students in the classroom can be distracting to you. Another disadvantage is if the teacher uses videos and visuals to teach you then it will also be difficult to be able to retain the information that you're trying to learn. Another disadvantage is that even though audio materials are found on the internet opponents that say auditory learning with audio materials isn't helpful, say that it's actually hard in classrooms because if the teacher provides you reading materials instead then it's going to be difficult for you to learn without reading that material out loud.

This is something that you can't do if you're in a class full of people unless you want to be rude. Even whispering could disturb others. This learning style is also limited in terms of the learning environment that you can use because a cafe or a noisy environment where you wouldn't be able to hear the recording isn't going to help you either and you can also disrupt other learners because you have to hear the information because that's the best way for you to be able to absorb if for yourself. Because a student in a classroom would have to whisper or read the materials out loud if you're not able to listen to it through headphones this wouldn't be advisable unless you are in a location alone where you can speak aloud.

Kinesthetic learner:

The third learner on this list is what is known as the kinesthetic learner. A kinesthetic learner is a learner that is someone who is hands on and someone who learns best by doing things. This is a very interesting type of learner because they don't learn the way that others on this list do and it's completely different. The other three learners on this list have some similarities but this one is set apart a little bit and it's quite interesting to see how they are able to learn things and how quickly that they are able to pick up the information that is being presented to them in their careers or at their job.

What this means for a kinesthetic learner is that they don't learn best by just sitting at a desk and repeating information or seeing information on a chart. What they need to do to learn at the best of their ability and to be able to learn things easier is that they need to be able to get up. What this means for them is that they actually have to do whatever it is they're trying to learn. There are other ways that they can learn but this is the best way for them to do this. As in some areas of your work this isn't feasible, we have listed the other way that a kinesthetic learner is able to obtain information and retain it as well.

An example of what you should do to help a learner of this type is the following. A great idea for a learner this that learns this way would be to put a few exercises in place. Imagine that you're going to a meeting and you have a table of employees. Or you could imagine that you're in a presentation and that you have a large audience. Either way what you can do for these types of learners is that you can let your audience stand up and let them move around for a bit. This helps their learning capabilities and helps them with being able to learn and retain information.

For the people that work in your company to move around or even just being able to move around on your own if you are this type of learner is going to give you the opportunity to learn more and how you need to. You need to demonstrate and experience whatever it is that you're trying to learn. If you learn better by the ability to move and the ability of doing what you need to do, you actually have to be able to be in a position where you're able to get up and try to learn what it is you're trying to learn. If your company or place of work doesn't allow this, there is another way that these learners can learn which gives them a similarity to the last learner on this list.

If you're not able to do this then you should be aware that as a kinesthetic learner you can learn by being able to write things down in order to remember and retain important information that is going to help you. A big part of being effective at your job is learning how to remember and learn as well as grow in your field. You have to be willing to try. So for this learner moving is obviously the best way that they could learn but if you don't have that option then you have to be able to have a backup plan so that your still able to be successful and effective in your job. Productivity is one of the important skills you need to master as well and if your able to identify you're learning style; it's going to be able to help you achieve this because it lets you know yourself better.

In addition to what we've already covered here is some additional information about kinesthetic learners. These learners are the ones who prefer to learn by direct experience or physical learning as we've said before but regardless of an individual's preferred learning style they can still benefit from this learning approach because research has shown that this learning style results in increased learning outcomes from all students. You can reap the benefits of that for yourself. Evidence has also shown that this type of learning will not only improve your intelligence, but it will also help in helping people be able to reach the necessary levels of physical activity which they need on a daily basis.

This can prevent major health problems later on in life or even in their current state including heart disease. Kinesthetic learning should appeal to more than just individuals looking for their learning style. It should appeal to more than just people who are already kinesthetic learners as well because this learning style can appeal to anybody who struggles with cooperation, coordination or social skills in their life because it offers multiple benefits for all learners.

Kinesthetic learning activities can help remove stress fear or feelings of failure because these learning activities are meant to inspire determination, creativity and focus while letting you have fun. This means that letting kinesthetic learners use these activities is going to be able to help them learn and grow the way that they need to.

Reading and writing learners:

The ability to write things down helps these learners just not as much as the first way that we've listed. It's just not the first and only thing that helps them learn. It may be a backup idea for how to help them learn, but one important thing to remember is that it can be placed at the forefront if that is what is able to help this learner reach their maximum potential and learn better and at their best. If something doesn't work for a particular type of reader we have to be willing to try something new if what we're doing doesn't work. Resilience is key in making your skills work together and to keep reaching for success. Failure isn't forever and remember that you should keep trying no matter what.

The last type of learner on this list is known as the reading and writing learner. Reading is very important, and it has been stressed in the business world, the academic world and it's a hobby for people around the globe. Writing is much the same. It is an important part of the business world and you need to be able to utilize these skills if you don't have them and your one of the people that learn better this way, you're in luck.

For this type of learner they do best as the title implies, by reading and by writing. These types of learners are able to do their best when they are able to read or when they are offered the ability to write. When they are able to both that offers a double benefit to this type of learner. If you want to help them learn or want to know what the best option for yourself to learn is the following.

The ability to be able to interact with text is more beneficial for them then seeing images or hearing the information like the first two learners on this list. Images don't necessarily help reading and writing learners either because they read and write better as their title implies. Because this is what helps them learn better for these types of people, the best way to help you learn would be written quizzes. Most people hate quizzes and avoid them like the plague. For this type of learner it is very beneficial because they can use both of their skills at the same time.

Quizzes give you a chance to read the information that they want you to learn and then utilize the writing skills that you have to write the information which shows you that you'll be able to remember the information. It also lets you see if you have been able to retain the information that you've studied and how you can improve if you don't do as well as you would like too.

Other options are that when you are writing and you have an exercise that lets you do so, you have the opportunity or chance to write down what it is you're thinking. This is a great way for people to be able to express themselves while they are learning. In other cases it helps you see what it is you have been able to study and learn over time.

Another helpful way for reading and writing learners to learn the best for themselves is if you're presented with a handout of what the company or job is trying to get you to learn. Then you can read the handout and write down what you were able to learn from it. This also works in a presentation as well. Any project of a company or job can really be adapted to this type of learning. If they try they could adjust their meetings or styles to any of these types of learnings with very little trouble.

The reason that this helps is that if you have a project or anything of that nature then you can read it out loud and see and be able to absorb the information because you're actually being able to read it in your head or out loud. Many people are able to do this at their own pace which is another benefit that is really going to be able to help you in the long run and help you to get better at learning this way and use it to your advantage to further your career and aspirations.

Other helpful hints about reading and writing learners are the following. Reading and writing learners need reading materials so that they can take points that they think are important from what they hear, see or read. They have the advantage of making students more independent because they can do it on their own. With note taking they retain more of the concepts on their own without any help and they have a learning style that works for them. They also faced a disadvantage however, because if you only have visual instruction or an audio instruction and they don't have access to reading materials or writing materials, they might find that the situation is harder and that can cause issues when they are trying to learn.

Study advice for reading and writing learners that will help in their jobs, careers, or their professional lives are that they should read of course and that they should rewrite the notes that they have. This is helpful if you're going to be trying to be able to retain the information. While you are rewriting you should remember also that you should take lots of notes during class or in a meeting, because textbooks don't capture the same information and the same feel of what the student is taught in a classroom. Taking lots of notes in a meeting will accomplish the same thing. A handout, though effective, is not the same as writing notes from the meeting itself so that you can remember the feel and vibe from the meeting as well as anything the speaker said that wasn't in the handout.

Doing this means that your more prepared for you job and it's more beneficial to you later when your restudying and making sure you've got the information you need. Another thing that is very important is to be sure not to lose the handouts that your teacher, your job or your company gives you. If you are careless with the handouts and don't pay attention to where you put them, you can't study the information and if tested chances are you could fail.

This is going to help make sure that you're more prepared for your career and that you're understanding what your job wants you to do so losing them should be something to avoid at all costs. Using bullet points is also very helpful for reading and writing learners and instead of having a chart or diagram you can turn it into words because that's the learning style that works best for you.

You can also determine whether or not you're a reading and writing learner in the first place. If you enjoy reading and you find that you work best in a quiet area these are both signs that this could be your style. If you prefer to study or work alone to avoid distraction or if you would rather read by yourself instead of having someone else read to you these are also signs. Maybe you're just someone who takes verbatim notes when someone's talking to you. These are all characteristics that you might be a reader writer learner as well.

These options are what is really going to make a difference in these types of learners in their lives and careers and it is what is going to help those types of learners achieve their best. They need the ability to be able to write out how they're feeling or what they're thinking with the ability to be able to read what it is they need to know. When these two options are combined, these types of learners are said to thrive and do better for themselves.

When you enter the career that you're choosing for yourself or when you're trying to find a new career if your skills are not needed anymore, then it's best to know what type of learner you are so that you know how you're able to function at your best. As a generalist you'll have many different skills that you're good at and you may even be able to cross over into different learning styles as time passes on.

Many people have learned later on in life and later in their careers that while they thought they were one type of learner they may have crossed over into being another type of learner as they get older. If this happens that's fine. People grow and change in their lives and need to be able to understand that and be adaptable to themselves so that they can improve.

Other people share similarities between different types of learning. There are people that are reading and writing learners, but they find that their actually able to learn visually as well. This may sound confusing or odd, but this does happen. Most people do fall into one of these four categories but as everybody's different some people fall in between two of the categories and they might find that they are a good cross between two as well.

Whatever you're learning style is that you have been able to discover for yourself it's important that you learn it for yourself so that you're able to take your career even further and that your able to take yourself further in your personal life. Learning how to adapt you're learning style into your life is also going to help you be able to learn how to stack your skills and bring yourself more success. This is what this book is trying to achieve for you and help you accomplish. This book is trying to tell you how it is that you can use your different skills to gain success in your life and by following the tips in this chapter you will be able to find more success in your career as a result.

Chapter six: Meta Skills- What They Are and Why You Need Them

Meta skills are in important thing that you will have to develop in order to achieve this goal of becoming a generalist and they're also just as important as becoming a specialist. In in this endeavor you want to become a generalist and we will go through the points of what meta skills are and how you can develop them for your benefit and why it's important to develop them for your benefit in your business life. Meta skills are skills that can be broken down into the following.

1.   Focus

2.   Discipline (this is going to include managing your time and productivity)

3.   Memory techniques

4.   Persuasion (or people skills)

5.   Writing

These five skills are what you're going to need to know in order to be successful in any field you choose. A meta skill is essentially a high order skill that enables and empowers other skills to happen. So basically what it is, is the foundation on what you're going to be able to engage new skills with. There are many different meta skills from confidence, to critical thinking, empathy and self-awareness. Some of these are considered to be soft skills but they are anything but. Some of these abilities are going to be able to help in everything you do and if you apply all of these to every facet of your life you will be more successful. Empathy is very important in a business world and in the personal world that you are going to be living in and confidence is key in the business world as well. So these definitely are not soft skills.

They are very good skills that you're going to need to master. Knowing how to learn is what is going to allow everything else to happen for you. The development of important meta skills are derived from your ability to learn. You can go and study techniques that will help you learn your meta skills better. You could try experimenting and developing different explanations for understanding your skills as well. Other ideas to try are that you could practice and apply your knowledge to the real thing, whether it is a task or for a test. Just exhibit what you know when you're trying to apply your meta skills to the real world. You could read information about the meta skills or explain to other people what you think those skills are but in this chapter we're going to cover what they are and why they're important to you. Or at least why they should be important to you. Embrace learning. The ability to learn comes from the mindset that you're in while you're trying to learn. You have to be able to understand that you're walking into unknown territory and there are questions and you need the answers but when you start out you're a beginner. Remember that this is fine. Everyone starts out as a beginner so the first thing you need to understand is to understand that you're going to be vulnerable and that you're going to begin the journey toward learning as a novice. You have to get more comfortable with it and follow your curiosity to new ideas and fields. Understand that the more curious you are the more you going to be wanting to learn. The more you're wanting to learn the better you're going to be. Don't be afraid of technology and don't procrastinate. Be sure to learn what you can while you can.

There are another 5 meta skills that will cause you to succeed in your career and in your life. These skills are the following.

1. Learning. Which is the autodidactic ability to learn new skills.
2. Dreaming. Which is the meta skills that is with applied imagination.
3. Seeing. which is the ability to think entire thoughts which is also known as system thinking.
4. Feeling. Which include social intelligence, intuition, and using your empathy.
5. Making. Which means the mastering of design processes which include devising

prototypes or including the skills for devising prototypes if you don't have them already

Other meta skills include the following as well.

1. Self-awareness. This is the ability to have an accurate view of your own abilities, your shortcomings and skills. It has a more positive impact on leadership than an MBA or other things of that nature. Self-awareness encourages people to be able to lead themselves with authenticity and integrity which in turn makes them better leaders and they're also more empathetic as well as being able to accept reality better.

2. Creativity is another skill that you will need and it's more than developing original ideas. It's about exploring different ways of solving problems. Creative people who are more creative are better with improvisation, they are also better at problem solving and they have more innovation. Many organizations have approached

innovation and with a mentality of certainty. They believe that the right process is able to uncover the right solution, but the right process is different for other people and creativity and innovation embraces experimentation instead of perfection. It also embraces empathy instead of being an egomaniac and the art of doing instead of planning.

3. Resilience is another skill that is going to serve you well. Failure is apart of any business and in any life and being able to rise above it and to keep trying is a useful skill that you need to develop. Overcoming failure in your life requires more than just being open minded. Overcoming failure takes constant experimentation but it can take a toll on a team because it takes patience and time to experiment in the first place. That's why most people give up after a couple of attempts but remember this. Thomas Edison failed hundreds of times

before he created a light bulb that people could use and that functioned properly. That mentality and understanding that you can fail before you succeed is going to help you in the long run with your business and your life. It doesn't have to be a bad thing. It just means you keep trying. Resilience means that you rise above adversity and you have learned that making mistakes doesn't have to be forever. If you're able to use all of these skills to your benefit your team will be stronger, more adaptable and it will have a stronger leader.

To the original 5 skills that we mentioned, we will now discuss persuasion. Persuasion is an important meta skill to have because if you're not able to talk to people and communicate with them effectively, then you're not going to go very far in business. Even people who sit behind a screen have to talk to people eventually so having good communication skills is going to save you from having very awkward times and it's going to be able to get you promoted to where you need to be. Remember that in the business world effective communication is the most important thing. If you're not able to do this then you need to learn how to do it so that you'll be able to achieve what it is you're wanting to achieve to go further in your career and in your life.

Persuasion is considered to be an art and it is one of the most important things you can learn for the business world. Remember that in the business world you need to be able to hold conversations with people. You also need to be able to have leadership skills and make sure that if your company is in sales that you can do this effectively. Anything that requires influencing others is where persuasion comes in and you need to be able to do this effectively.

Writing is another important business tool on this list that we will be talking about. The reason that you're going to have to learn how to this is that writing is that it is in every aspect of the business world whether you think it is or not. You need to be able to do this effectively because it's another way that you will need to communicate with your clients, your business and even your family and friends. Because of all of this you're going to need to understand how to do this and put in a bit of work if you can't. Writing makes your job easier to do. It also makes your thoughts and feelings easier to express. This is a skill that will make you more successful in the business world as well as being able to communicate better with others. Many people still haven't been able to do this so you will be ahead of others who are trying to do the same job or field that you are.

The next skill on this list is memory techniques. Memory techniques are important because they help you retain the information that your trying to make sure that you can use to your advantage. With a good memory you can not only obtain new knowledge, but you will be able to retain it as well. There are many memory techniques that you can use for your benefit and the first is a spaced repetition system. As we will discuss later in this book this method is a very good technique for making sure that information will stay with you. If you hear that Sacramento was the capital of California and you were tested on that same day, you'd get an A. If you were tested a couple of weeks down the road you probably wouldn't. This is why you should use spaced repetition learning.

Spaced repetition depends on how many cards you view each day when your studying. Some people find that flash cards are very useful, and this memory technique is very effective for you. You can accelerate you're learning and from there you'll be able to obtain more information on much quicker level for your job. You can get compound benefits from the knowledge that you will be obtaining now because the more you know, the more easily you'll be able to learn. Your new knowledge of new topics and subjects and other things make links between different areas of knowledge to come up with different solutions. This helps with creative minds as well because as we've mentioned above creative minds are able to come up with novel solutions in their jobs, companies and personal lives. Psychologists have recently studied and reviewed the best learning methods and they have found that practice testing and distributed practice along with spaced repetition were at the top when combined. This is where you use practice sessions over time rather than cramming all at once. By using this memory technique in the ways that we have listed you can see benefits and you'll be able to start realizing that you're learning much more than used to. You will also be able to obtain more information and you'll see that you remember information much more clearly.

Discipline is another meta skill you need and this one is important as well. discipline is a single word in the vocabulary but it's different for every country across the globe. For example in the country of America everybody talks about it and everybody wants it but a lot of people in this culture act like they are completely hating it and avoid it. Many act like they want nowhere near it. They don't want to do it, and this is happening all over. It's becoming more and more obvious that discipline is needed in our lives. The plan is something that we need to work on. We want skills and will chase after what we think is the best possible choice for us but sometimes we forget that nothing comes without discipline. Think about when you were younger. Your parents try to teach you discipline because they felt like you would be at a serious handicap without it. People teach people discipline in martial arts or jobs or in anything that you try because they know that you need the discipline to do this the right way, not just for the job or for your career or a hobby but for yourself . We all believe that we have special talent and special skills and we do but what we lack in our lives is the discipline to turn it into anything we can actually use. If we have skills without discipline, the skills that we have tried so hard to learn are going to waste. This is because few of us actually know what to do with the skills we have and there are very few of us that actually do anything good with the skills that we have. We need to be good at what we do and if you're not naturally good at what you do, there's nothing wrong with that. The only thing that means is that you have to work to get good at it. We need the discipline to build those skills into something that we can use and something that's going to help us in our life.

Now we have said that a specialist uses discipline to master one particular skill and they don't care how long it takes. A generalist is good at many different things, but they still need discipline to do something with those skills and they still need discipline to make themselves good with those skills. No skill can be mastered without discipline behind it.

Disciplining ourselves in our daily lives isn't the easiest task that needs to be done for ourselves, but it is one of the biggest things we can do for ourselves to benefit our professional lives and our personal ones as well. The main thing that we have to do is eliminate distractions. Distractions are all around us and we even create distractions for ourselves because we don't want to get things done or because the task at hand is unpleasurable. This isn't even a conscious thing for some people. We don't want to do the unpleasurable task, so we create other tasks to fill up our time. In the business world this is grounds for getting fired in certain cases. What this method of distracting your self is called is creative distracting. This means your filling your time with non-essential tasks that we don't need to do at the moment instead of what we actually need to do. This can also be known as procrastination. If you're in a field like writing for example then you understand what procrastination is and the fact that you do a multitude of other things before doing what you need to do.

This is unhealthy for you because all your doing is serving to make sure that you can't finish your projects in a timely manner and your projects may not be getting done at all depending on your distraction level. You could also be stressing yourself out for no reason because your upset that you can't finish your projects on time. A sense of discipline is needed to make sure that you are able to do your projects on time. One way of beginning to discipline yourself is to set deadlines for yourself if necessary and you can eliminate the distractions in your life or at least limit them so that they're not affecting you in a negative way. You need to make it a habit of saying that you'll do what you need to do and that you'll actually do what you're saying you're going to do. You have to condition yourself to change and condition yourself to understand that you actually need to keep your word to others and to yourself.

Focus does not get the respect that it needs from our world or the business world and it should. We hear a lot about other things that we need for our jobs like leadership and team culture as well as emotions and the stress that that the business world can cause. We don't hear much being placed on how much focus is important and the ability that it plays in our role to be productive. We also don't hear about how important it is to the business world, but it is. In fact focus is one of the most important parts to the business world.

Focus involves your ability to pay attention to things that are going to help you and focus is the ability to avoid things that aren't going to help you like distraction. If you're going to finish a project for example, then you need to focus on vital information and the analysis's that would finish the project. One of the most important things that you need to avoid is distractions such as the television, your computer, or the people around you.

All of these things can cause distractions and focus is a very important skill to learn because without it you can't think properly. Focusing is important to every aspect of thinking and in particular, it's important to memory learning, it's important to problem solving, reasoning and perception as well as the ability to make decisions. If you don't have good focus every aspect of your ability to think is going to suffer which is going to affect how your able to work.

You won't be as effective in your work and it will affect you in ways you hadn't thought of. When you can't focus you are not concentrating on the things that you need to be concentrating on and you won't be concentrating on getting your work done. Which means that you won't be capable of doing so and you won't be giving your maximum effort because your mind is going to be wandering and you're going to be wasting time. This means that you're not going to be as productive and your company is going to think that you're not serious about the job.

The key then would be to focus better. This is going to be helpful to your job and in your life. If you can declutter your mind and minimize your distractions then you'll find that you can focus better. If you like most other businesspeople have tasks throughout your day that you need to get done, then what you should be doing for yourself and for your career is to begin to learn how to prioritize your tasks and then take on that list step by step. Take on the smaller steps first if your intimidated. Take small steps to accomplish what you need to, and you'll find that you have more energy for the bigger tasks that you have.

The less clutter you have in your mind the better that you're going to be able to focus. This is something that many studies have been conducted on and the results have come out that if you are able to create a focused workspace and get rid of unnecessary clutter that you will be able to work better. This is because if you can create a focused workspace that will help you in another way as well. A workspace filled with clutter means that your mind has unnecessary distractions and to help you focus better you should simplify your office and remove everything that doesn't need to be there.

You can keep some family photos on your desk to make your office space more inviting and less depressing (because many people say that cubicles can get depressing and there's no color or anything that helps your mood, you can improve your mood with little touches), but you don't need to have everything on your desk. For example you don't need to have a stack of magazines on your desk and you don't need to have old food on your desk either. You need a clean space in order to work and work properly.

The most difficult obstacle for any businessperson is the mastering of technology and this is going to be on area of focus that is vitally important for you and your career. It's ever changing, and you need to be able to keep up with it for your job and this can create stress in your job which means that you need to be able to focus all the more. Another distraction with technology is all of the messages and notifications that you get throughout the day. Even the least busy person will get notifications throughout the day.

All of those pings and notifications that let you know that you have a voicemail or text message are going off while you're trying to concentrate, and these sounds can serve as a constant distraction. People who are great multitasker's have claimed that they are great at the ability to focus. They have claimed that all of their focus goes to the tasks and that they are able to do each and every task with ease because of their ability to focus.

Others have said that those people that claim to be the best multitaskers have actually been proven to be the worst multitaskers. Many other people believe that there's actually no such thing as multitasking at all when it comes to work and that you shouldn't call yourself a multitasker because it can be negative. The choice is ultimately yours as the research on the subject has been going back and forth for years. Some studies have shown that people are able to be multitaskers, and some have shown that they can't. In this everchanging world, there's always more information that we need to be able to make an informed decision so for now we will have to wait until more information comes out on the subject.

With the distractions of technology at work one of the best things that you can do to help yourself is to turn off each and every piece of technology and force yourself to get to work and focus on the task at hand. If you have to leave your technology on because things are going on with your family, your home, or your worried about an emergency, then put it on vibrate. Just make sure that this doesn't violate your companies phone policy. The business world is usually more accepting of phones because you need it for work, but each company is different and has different policy's, so you need to be sure of which one your individual company has. If not, you could get in trouble.

If you able to turn off your technology or at least put it on vibrate your less aware of the sounds going on around you because in most cases a vibrate is soft. The only downside to putting your phone on vibrate is that you can't tell which notification you're getting whereas with sound you can. But either way, turning the technology off is making sure that you're not getting distracted by their constant sounds going off and you will be able to focus on the work you have and the tasks at hand.

Remember that you need to perform in your life and in your job and if you're constantly distracted then you can't do that.

The reason, or at least one of them, that you need to focus in the workplace is that you need to have the ability to be able to process what's going on around you and you need to be present. This means that you are focusing on what's in front of you. Another way to say this is that your concentrating on the here and now. You're getting involved in your job and you also need to be productive which means focusing only on the things that are important and blocking out what's not.

If you're able to take control of your ability to focus and make sure that you're focusing better, then you've done something for yourself that can change your entire life. The ability to focus helps your career and can open you up to new opportunities like promotions and new experiences because your company will see that your able to take this job seriously and that your making the effort to improve yourself. This goes a long way with companies, and they like to see that your taking the effort to try and make yourself better.

To be able to train your mind to focus is to be able to give yourself a powerful tool that will enable you to perform at a much higher level and you'll be consistently better and more effective as well. This will mean that you are able to be a much more efficient worker in your work efforts for your career in whatever field you have chosen for yourself. In addition this also means that you're going to have a better work attitude because you'll be more successful and a better quality of life. The ability to focus will also give you the opportunity to better achieve your professional goals because you've learned how to focus. Not to mention that the ability to focus can be skill stacked with many other skills which will open even more doors for you as time goes on. Remember that the ability to stack your skills is going to work in your favor in the business world because it takes you further. Companies are looking for people who have good skills that can be put to use and if you

put in the time and effort the person
that they are looking for will be you.

Chapter seven: Accelerated Learning Techniques

Some accelerated learning techniques will be able to help you on this road to bettering yourself for your career and your personal life as well. Accelerated learning techniques are techniques that you can use to learn skills faster than normal. An example would be if you're trying to learn a skill that would normally take years, decades or even longer to study and accelerated learning techniques will help you learn it much faster as long as you have the right mind set in place going into it.

The most important thing that you can do for anything in your life is to make sure that you have adopted the right attitude. Before you begin accelerated learning you need to have a positive and resourceful state of your mind. If you begin learning or studying with a negative mental state your virtually setting yourself up to fail. Your body needs to work with positivity and so does your mind. With that being said the first thing that you need is to be able to have a good mental state and be positive and understand that this is going to help you in the long run. Negative emotions can make you depressed and unable to think or concentrate so you need to try and keep your mood happy and strong. It can be hard to stay in a positive head space, but it will benefit you more when you are able to do it.

Another thing that you're going to be able to do for yourself is you need to make sure that the information is able to stay with you and will discuss how you're going to be able to do this in this chapter. You'll need to be able to demonstrate what you've learned from yourself and others and you'll have to be able to make sure that you can reward yourself for being smart by making good choices for yourself and learning what you need to do for yourself. To make sure that you are able to keep this information with you, you'll need to be sure to follow the steps in this chapter so that you'll be able to understand the best way to use these tips and make sure that you're able to keep using them for your advantage.

The first thing that you can learn to do is break difficult ambitions or big goals into smaller and more achievable goals. Many people confuse having ambitions with having goals. For example, learning how to speak Japanese would be an ambition. Meaning that this is something that somebody wants to do. If you said I want to learn the most conversational phrases in Japanese, that is different. That is a measurable and achievable goal. The key to being able to enhance your capabilities for learning is to be able to break down all of your ambitions, and it doesn't matter if they're related to health, your personal life, business or any other area, you need to break them up into a series of measurable and smaller goals. Smaller goals are easier to achieve than bigger goals because they take less time though both are possible and achievable.

Many people also understand the importance of focusing effectively on one thing at once and then if they desire to do so trying to learn how to do 2 things at once. After you have broken down your goal, you need to be able to focus on one thing at a time. As we've already focused on the issue of focus in another chapter we won't delve too much into it here, but we do need to tell you that you need to block out distractions. Instead of watching YouTube and checking your email and spending all of your energy during other things which is doing nothing except prolonging your task because you're not concentrating on it, you need to work on a single task at one time for maximum productivity for yourself.

If you need help blocking the noise turn off your phone. If you're worried about having an emergency then put your phone on vibrate. As we've said before however the only thing bad about doing so is that it will be difficult when you put your phone on vibrate to understand what type of notifications are going off. It will however give you the ease of mind of knowing that if there's an emergency they can still read you. However you don't need other distractions. You don't need to have books or magazines on your desk when you should be working, and you don't need to have your computer on the internet or on video sharing sites. Staying away from social media or messaging your friends as well. You should be focused on work and making sure that you are doing what you need to do instead.

Another accelerated learning technique that you'll be able to use is the principle known as the 80/20 rule. Many people are familiar with the 80/20 rule from watching Tyler Perry's movies. They apply the 80/20 rule to marriage. You're going to apply the 80/20 rule to work and business. It's a simple rule that means that 80% of your results will come from 20% of your work. It's mostly used in the business world for sales. For example 80% of your sales would be coming from 20% of your customers but in reality it can be applied to anything like it was in the movie. Basically in English 20% of your words make up 80% of the of written language. Music is the same. Accelerated learning requires that you focus on the vital 20% and avoid wasting time on the less vital 80%

of the task. You can apply this principle to any learning that you're going to do for yourself.

It doesn't matter if you're trying to learn a foreign language or if you're trying to learn computer programming or even if you're just trying to learn things faster than you do now. Instead of focusing on the 80%, you need to focus on the vital 20% because that's where you going to be able to get your results.

Mind maps are another powerful tool that you can use for accelerated learning. A mind map is a great way to learn new skills that you would like to be able to master. It's really easy to break them down into smaller steps of study as well as revision and practice. Remember that revising, repeating and practicing is going to make you better at learning. We will tell you more about practice and repetition later on in this book so we're not going to talk too much about it here. We're just going to say that you can use mind maps to solve different problems and break down complex systems into simple processes and small processes. You can also just deconstruct a complicated task that you have. The benefits of using mind maps have been proven to be huge from improved organizational skills, to being able to have a deeper and more practical understanding of any topic that you're trying to learn about.

You should also break your work into small sessions. This is a way to make sure that your cognitive skills and mentality aren't getting burned out. If you feel burned out at the end of your workday you're not alone. Most people feel that they work far more effectively when they're able to have small sessions of maybe 25 minutes to an hour of work. They say they work better doing this than a solid 4 to 5, or 6 to 9 hours of work that's constant and hands on. Everyone is different however, so remember that some people do work better when they're working 9 hours straight and they don't have any time to rest.

Other people find that breaking up their work throughout the day is better for their mental state and it's better for their mental abilities and learning styles.

Regardless of how efficient your skills are if you struggle to develop the skills in the first place it's most likely because you lack motivation and energy to continue and to go on. Stress and cognitive burnout can be a serious issue especially if you're going to be learning these skills over a lifelong period of time. One of the best ways to avoid is burnout, however, is by using the 80/20 rule that we've discussed above and to break your learning sessions into smaller manageable times slots. This is going to let you be able to take a break if you need it and make sure that you're not burning yourself out or stressing yourself unnecessarily.

once you've learned a new skill you need to be able to reactivate it every time you need it. We compare skills to riding a bike in most cases and this is especially true in the business world. Once the skill is learned it's almost impossible to forget them but you're not going to be using them all the time. Other skills like the ones based around knowledge are very easy to unlearn and it's actually surprisingly easy how fast you can unlearn it. Reactivating a skill whether it's speaking a different language or playing an instrument is simple. All you have to do is relearn the skills that you forgot by using exercises to remember the fundamentals of that skill. That will help the rest come back to you naturally. A good example is if you want to relearn a language, all you have to do, since you already know the language, is simply rematch a foreign TV show without subtitles and you'll probably be able to remind yourself of how to do this quicker than you thought.

You should also collaborate with your friends because that's a great way to test your knowledge and abilities. If you're a competitive person this is perfect for you because you can set challenges up for yourself and it's a great way to improve and accelerate the process of learning anything you want. To help you focus on the process of learning anything, you can work with your friends to test each other's abilities and then you can acquire all new skills together. You can have a vocabulary competition if you're trying to learn something new for work or become bilingual for a better job, or you can measure your progress in the weight room if you're trying to lose weight. These are both good examples to make this clearer for you. Healthy competition has been proven to be a great way to be able to accelerate the process and learning of new skills.

Be sure to take time to smell the roses. Anyone with a 9 to 5 job can attest that most of their productive work occurs during the morning and they feel tired during afternoon. Others can agree that when they come home they might just want to sleep because they feel burned out and tired from a long day. So what you should do is remember that most of us work better when we have maybe a 3 to 4, or 2 to 4 hour daily window. This window of productivity also applies to the ability to learn. The time we can spend learning something and the knowledge that were able to retain from learning something is more of a logarithmic curve. What this means is that in order to maximize those skills it's often important to work less than you think.

Focus on taking a break and letting the information you've acquired sink into your brain. This is better than cramming over and over endlessly into the night. If you need to take a break to avoid burnout then you should take a break to avoid burnout. It reduces stress and it will make you feel better so that you'll be able to study more in the future. It also means that you're able to retain the information that you're trying to use for yourself. Being able to see your progress will help you see if there is something you need to work on or something your falling behind on. Don't let yourself get down if you feel you've taken a step back. Just keep trying and know that you can do this and try your best. That is what will make things happen for you.

There have been many research studies done on sleep and there is actually a very large body of research that is able to suggest that sleep may be one of the most important factors of how were able to learn. How well we're able to learn if you sleep is affected as well. When you sleep after one of your learning experiences it is said that with a well-rested brain, you're able to have better focus and process new information. Another interesting fact to learn is that if you sleep following a learning experience that you have done for yourself, your brain is going to solidify the connections that it formed while you were learning. The activity in the brain while you're sleeping mirrors the activity during learning. This is especially true for new motor skills. So if you're wanting to know what that means, this means that your brain is practicing learning while you're sleeping.

Sleeping between sessions of learning is also helping to space learning out. This means if you're learning fast and using spaced learning as we talked about before, it is ultimately better to help ensure faster and better learning. We've already talked about testing yourself which is a bigger accelerated learning technique than most people realize because you're able to memorize and retain information better, but as we've talked about it in other chapters of this book we won't get too much into it here either.

Another accelerated learning technique is to connect the dots. If you can make the effort to draw connections and relationships between what it is you're learning and other things in your life, you should be able to achieve what is known as elaborative encoding. Elaborative encoding means that your memory has the ability to store, recall and encode information.

It basically means that you're allowing the perceived item of interest or whatever it is you that you're learning to be converted into something that can be stored within your brain. So if you're connecting the dots and using things like pneumonic then they should be able to make that encoding easier. An example of this is a musician. Many musicians when they are learning their keys is to follow the phrase 'every good boy does fine'. The reasoning behind this is that it helps you learn the notes on the treble clef. It's taught in many schools and it's taught in many colleges because this helps people who are learning music to understand it much better and much quicker. In most schools if you're playing music you need to learn your keys and a song within a week. Accelerating your learning is vital then.

If you're teaching a new concept and trying to learn it, you should spend time reflecting on it and visualizing how it might apply to your day to day life. This is another form of encoding. In most people's experience if they're able to put the effort into connecting the dots it doesn't feel that much like you're having fun. It is going to feel like work. The amount of time that you're dedicating to it doesn't have to be as large as you think. Even just a few minutes of elaboration or trying to encode during the day can have a tremendous experience and a tremendous difference in how much and how fast are able to learn.

Tracking your progress is also a great idea to accelerate you're learning. Any athlete or businessperson can tell you that anytime they have a goal for themselves they're going to be tracking their progress to see if they are actually being able to achieve what they're trying to achieve. They also want to see if they are getting better at what they're trying to do. You can do this too. Make sure that you're on the right track and that your succeeding and moving forward.

As much as you possibly can be sure to immerse yourself in the environments where you're learning. Make sure that you can immerse yourself in the areas where your learning will be able to be ultimately applied. This is a very well-known approach for language learning and that's vital in the business world. If you live in a country or you're visiting one for an extended period of time, which many businesses do because they have to go overseas for business meetings and gaining new clients, putting your efforts in this situation and context as much as possible can provide a very powerful application and exposure to make sure that you're supplementing your conscious effort. This helps you learn better and to put yourself in many other learning situations where you can learn better. If you put yourself in this context you may not even know this, but you won't even have to leave your house. There's role playing games and there's other learning experiences like technology enhanced learning experiences that can bring those environments to you.

You shouldn't stuff your brain either. This may be considered a tip that is considered a non-tip, but cramming has been shown that it might hurt you more than help you. Cramming to get you through an exam doesn't help much with long term retention and real expert mastery. You do need to practice, repeat, review and practice and test yourself some more, but you should do this in spaced intervals. You need to study and practice for a while before stopping and then coming back to it later and maybe taking some sleep in between as we mentioned above.

Additional learning techniques that you can use for yourself is to understand that you need to be able to understand that accelerated learning is also trying to emphasize the wholeness and diversity Along with the individual nature and creativity of trying to help you learn and accelerated learning is to try and help you have a better state of mind.

Knowing that will be learning for the rest of our lives there are 5 additional accelerated learning techniques that have been found to be very effective in studies that have been performed.

Interleaved practice is an important skill that you're going to need to understand for yourself and what this means is mixing different kinds of problems together when you're studying. When you're studying something like math for example, you need to learn different kinds of formulas for different types of math. When you're learning one equation to compute the idea of a circle, you'll need to learn another to figure out the perimeter. The idea behind interleaved practice is that you're better at figuring out the problems if you're mixing some of the area problems. So when your mixing the area problems with the perimeter problems you should be able to study better.

The reason that this works for so many people is that they are able to learn a bit more about how to apply each formula. You'll need to learn how you can use these when you use another so that when you see a new problem you'll have to figure out what kind of problem it is. Many people think this is a useless skill to learn but what most people don't understand is that math as in every single thing that you do and every single job that you will ever have. By interleaving the problem that you have during your sessions while you're studying, you'll be able to give yourself practice and you'll be able to tell the problems apart much easier which will make learning much easier for you.

Another skill that you can use for yourself is self-explanation. The idea behind self-explanation is that it's a reading strategy and what it means is that you need to pause from reading information like a textbook or a series of information of papers that your boss will hand you set work, to study periodically and explain to yourself what it means to you. You should explain to yourself what you just read to see if you remembered what you read.

You can do this after a section of text, or you can do this after studying a problem. If you're trying to self-explain yourself, you may need to find that you didn't retain the information as well as you thought, and you have to go back over parts of whatever it is you're reading to fully understand what's being said. There have been professors that offer accounts and research of why this works and there have been many published books about why this works as well. The idea behind this is that it encourages you to make inferences based on what it is that you're reading. As you try to explain it to yourself you can also identify the problems and you can revise your explanations. This will serve to make sure that you're repairing your understanding but you're also enriching your understanding.

If you're going to go for the route of practice testing as we've mentioned before this is very helpful. You can make flashcards or simply answer questions from whatever it is that you need to study. You will often find free tests online for whatever it is that you're studying, and you should make sure that you can get the correct answers. Practice testing is able to work best when you can find out whether or not you got the answers right or wrong. Otherwise you can just guess and not realize that you're completely wrong and this would cause more harm to you than help. This isn't what you want. You want to accelerate you're learning not cause yourself unnecessary issues.

Another accelerated learning skill that can help you is called asking why. Another name for this is called elaborative interrogation. A great way to learn is to ask questions. When you were younger you probably asked a million different questions and you probably drove your parents crazy by doing so when they weren't able to come up with anything. This is a good thing however because it helped you learn and grow and that is going to help you here.

There are many children that don't hesitate to ask questions every single minute of every single day and their parents quickly find that they're running out of answers as we just started. This is something that's going to help you because there has been a great amount of research that has been done to show that this is something that is useful. If you can get yourself to answer questions that you are asking yourself, it's going to encourage you to integrate whatever new fact you've learned with things you already know. In a way this is mirroring skills stacking. This is going to improve your memory for the new fact by giving you more memory hooks and techniques to find it. Research has shown that this is an effective way of learning. If you try this for yourself you should find that you are able to learn much more quickly and they are able to obtain more information. You'll also be able to realize that if you are for getting information there's a good memory hook to help bring it back.

The last accelerated learning techniques that we are going to be able to help you are the following. Conceptual clarity is more often seen as a learning technique that is based on the activities of expediting the learning process. Conceptual clarity encompasses within itself an activity of learning, but it doesn't convey a true import of a concept that's objective is to teach the entire person in order to impart elements to learners. Studies have shown that this learning technique can be helpful for kinesthetic learning and intelligences through mind mapping, thinking skills, and other associated key terms to learning.

Memory hooks are another technique. This is based on a principle of using 2 different pieces of information to express the construction of a sentence through an interconnecting theme with words that are going to follow each other logically. It may sound odd but in order to make your mind succeed with improving your memory this is actually very helpful. A famous TV show from the nineties actually used a very popular memory hook that students began using in high school when they were studying for their finals. You can use this sort of memory hook to remember things in business as well. Everything in business needs to be remembered and everything at your job needs to be remembered as well.

If you're not able to have the knowledge of everything you need to know than your boss is going to find someone who can remember things and who can do them better on the tests the give you. The example we are going to use here is to remember that Eli Whitney is the person who invented the cotton gin. To remember Eli Whitney effectively you might think of something like Whitney Houston because Whitney is what you're trying to a remember. Whitney Houston is something easy to remember but the name Whitney will help you remember that Whitney was the last name of the person who invented the cotton gin. Memory hooks are very popular when you're trying to remember things and it can accelerate you're learning and your ability to remember things even faster.

Emotional display and calling things out loud follow 3 particular perceptibly sensors. The first is the aural and body movement as well as visuals. If the written material represents visual and hearing your voice, the body control is helped by hearing your voice.

You can also tell it a story. Stories are able to help us in more ways than we think, and they're actually ill shown as being able to impact the learning psyche of human beings. A vast array of the human activities that we do on a daily basis are based on stories and we tell stories in just about every setting that we are in. Examples include events like the following. If you're at a family gathering we tell a story, at office work we tell stories during the lunch hour, private conversations can turn into stories and even an individual person can create a story for themselves. The visual components are able to help your brain become sharp and this helps your brain become smarter and more imaginative through the creativity of telling the story.

While more studies do need to be known and conducted on how effective these last accelerated learning techniques are, there have been some studies that have said that they can be helpful for you. So they may be worth trying out for you if you feel like they can help you in your career and in your professional life.

One thing that is very helpful to remember in most cases is that different people have different styles of learning as we mentioned before. So if not all of the accelerated learning techniques that we've listed here work for you then that's fine. You have to use what works for you and what's going to be able to make you a better learner and better at obtaining this information. When we're learning other factors can affect us and knowing what other factors can affect us is a good idea to know. There are downsides to everything, and a lot of people say that there can be downsides to accelerated learning as well but for the most part many studies have agreed that accelerated learning is definitely able to help people learn quicker and to understand information a lot easier than they would if they didn't have these techniques at the ready.

Remember that you have to be motivated. One of the most important factors in anything that you do is motivation. If you're not motivated to do something then chances are you won't do it but if you are able to feel motivated then accelerated learning and being successful is going to help you in your career and life.

If you find that you're not able to find very many accelerated learning techniques on this list that can help you, we have offered more that you should be able to use for yourself in some area of your life.

Chapter eight: Practice and Repetition

Practice and repetition are very important to becoming a generalist, a specialist or even just becoming smarter in your everyday life. Many people express the need for wanting knowledge and wanting to learn new things and this is going to help you as a generalist in particular because you're trying to get many different skills to use. Not just one. A great example to make this clear to you is think back when you were in high school. This is going to help explain why practice and repetition are going to be so valuable to you. Every school since you were young has practiced repetition and the studying habits and benefits of repetition.

From elementary school until we have gone through high school and even in college, they tell you that flash cards are useful for repeating information. They also say that it is useful combined with studying. Another thing that they say is helpful is when you know the information and when you have repeated it over and over again it will help you remember this better than if you hadn't. In high school you have what is known as the end of the year finals or in college you have midterms. When you think about these tests, what you do when you have these tests coming into your life? You go home and then you open your textbooks before beginning to review all the information. Then you are most likely to write them on flash cards so that you can repeat the information to yourself and you can ask yourself the questions and answers until they've stuck in your brain.

When the next morning comes you would go to school the next day and you ace the test for the reason that you have repeated the information over and over until it stuck in your head. Another example is a song you hear on the radio. You hear it with your friends as you cruise down the street, you hear it in a store or even in a doctor's office. If it is a popular song chances are you will hear it a hundred times or more and the more times you hear it the more it sticks in your head.

The same is true with the information your studying. The information has been repeated so much it sticks in your head. This is one of the biggest reason practice and repetition is important for learning your skills and how they can help you learn what your needing to learn. Repetition is considered to be the mother of all learning. When you learned how to ride a bike or drive a car, anything you've ever done, you've had to learn the essential skills and you had to practice until you became better at it. This is the reason behind practice and repetition. Repetition can be used for reading as well as being able to be used for multisensory instruction.

It can be used in any type of learning that you're wanting to do. If you're using multi-sensory instruction the most effective way for people to learn is to engage in auditory, visual and action types of learning. For example, you need to see it, you need to hear it, and you need to do it. This will help you learn if your repeating the information over and over in your head or out loud. it

It's going to help you remember what it is you're learning. Repetition is a key learning aid because it will help transition skills from your conscious to your sub conscious through the repetition.

A skill is rehearsed over and over and practiced over time gradually becomes easier because you been used to doing it over and over and over again. As you improve you don't need to think consciously about what you're doing because you already know how to do it. This frees up your mind to learn how to do new skills and to understand new concepts. Practice alone doesn't make perfect. You should keep practicing the right way and you'll be able to do it right. Another important aspect of repetition is in the interval at which you're repeating. One of the best things about repetition is that many people can do this a different way as well. Including spaced repetition.

Spaced repetition means that you're learning a technique then incorporate increasing intervals of time between the practice of the previously learned material. So you space out the rehearsal of your task to make sure that the task sticks. This works especially well for learning vocabulary words in a foreign language or when you're trying to learn and absorbing bits of information that you need to know. Spaced repetition is also useful for factual knowledge as well. Since you have to learn these things for the business world practice repetition is definitely going to help you be able to achieve this for yourself.

The biggest reason that repetition helps us improve is because of the way that the cells in our brain communicate. The physical changes that they can undergo when they communicate repeatedly is why we should practice the same action over and over. Our brains are made up of neurons and neurons are what they call specialized cells. These specialized cells talk with each other and are able to communicate with each other using electrical signals that are called action potentials. When we perform an action for example, throwing a football, the neurons involved in that action are going to start firing signals or action potentials. What they do then is that they will begin to form an active network of cells. If you repeatedly practiced this action, you're increasing the Myleene around that said network. This leads to more efficient processing of cell signals and faster processing of the cell signals.

This leads to better performance. That's why spaced repetition is such a good practice and repetition is an important skill to utilize for yourself when we use space repetition what we're committing to memory at increasing intervals as we've said before, is information. The reason that this helps is because you're able to build that melene in your brain.

If you're consistently doing the wrong action for instance saying cat instead of hat, you're going to encode the information incorrectly. What that does to the neural pathways is that it makes them understand the incorrect action even stronger. As this is the opposite of being helpful, that's why you need to practice the right way and not the wrong way. If you follow the tips in this chapter you should be able to help your brain obtain information more easily and you should be able to remember the information more easily as well. This is going to offer you success in your career because you're going to be able to retain information that people are saying to you and testing you on much more easily. You'll be considered an asset to your company or your job.

Chapter nine: Conclusion

This book has been able to show you the benefits of being able to be a generalist over the benefits of being a specialist. Many people have heard arguments for and against both sides. We've shown how being a generalist is better than being a specialist due to today's demanding workloads and changing technology. You need to be able to have many different skills in order to keep up and not get lost in the shuffle. Remember that when you're a specialist you have one specific skill that you're an expert at. This means when they don't need you anymore or your skills anymore you can find yourself out of work or scrambling trying to find some. We have provided a solid argument and facts for providing information on this to let you know exactly why one is better than the other and why it is that area that you should focus on instead. Even if one skill in a generalist's arsenal is obsolete, they find another to fall back on. For this reason above many other's generalists are considered to be the better option for people. To prove that this is true we have offered solid examples of celebrities that are generalists and all the different places they've been able to use their talent. We've shown examples of entrepreneurs, singers, actors, and even a vice president of the United States and CEO of a major company.

This book has been able to provide you with examples of how people changed their entire world even though they started out as normal people just like us and how they were able to use what they had and used their passions to take themselves even further than they thought they could go. They were able to excel in what they did because they never gave up and they continued to have a positive attitude and understand that as long as they kept trying they would be able to make themselves successful. It doesn't happen overnight. But if you're willing to put in the time and effort it can happen for you just like it happens for everyone else. Just never give up on yourself and always have hope because there is something greater out there for everyone. By following their lead you will be able to find success in your own life as well as in your career and you will be able to use the skills from this book to make your own success. In anything that you do in life and in any job that you have or that you want, you need your company to be able to know what they have in you. Moreover, you want them to know why they made a good choice in hiring you. Using these tips is going to make that exact thing happen for you.

These people were able to not only excel in the field that they were trying to achieve, but they also were able to have success in the fields of philanthropy, writing, clothing, perfume and even the video game industry as well as healthcare. Some of the most successful businessmen and women on this list have been so successful because they understood that they needed to be in different fields to maximize their success and to be able to attempt different ventures for themselves. They realized they didn't have to stay in one field because their passions had extended so much further than that. They wanted to make something happen for their lives and they did.

They also understand what it is that the people want and how to give it to them. this is a useful trick to anyone in sales and marketing. When you show up to a job interview you know what the requirements are and what you need to do. This is the same concept. One businessman even has his company in the center of 400 other avenues. This means even if one idea doesn't work he still has plenty more. As such he is one of the most successful businessmen in the country and everyone knows who he is.

We've listed the ways they have been able to be successful because of the knowledge that they were able to use to their advantage. They understood that to be a great generalist you need to understand skill stacking. By now you know that this is the art of learning specific skills to achieve a goal. When you successfully combine your skills in this way you will be successful in your career and with the goals that your trying to achieve for yourself. Utilizing the information in this book is going to be able to help you do the same for your life. When people learn what these terms mean and how to achieve them, they are more equipped to do so because they have the skills. Another way to help yourself become successful is to learn what the different learning styles are. In most cases there are four and we go over them in detail so that you can see which one you relate to in your personal life. We let you know how they will help you achieve success and take you further than you have been able to go before.

We also teach you about Meta skills. Meta skills are something that many people haven't become overly familiar with and were taking the time to make sure that you are aware of what they are and how they can help; you. As we have outlined in this book the Meta skills that you need to know are the following. Memory techniques, focus, persuasion and people skills, and discipline. All of these are necessary skills to ensure success and help you develop real skills that are going to help you bring yourself knowledge and success later in your life. We have explained how to utilize each skill for your benefit and why they are so important to learn.

Many people also forget to take advantage of accelerated learning techniques and why practice is important. You've heard the expression practice makes perfect. Use that saying here and practice your skills and repeat the process. This is going to help you learn even faster and make sure that your able to actually use what you've learned to your advantage. Repetition may be boring, but it has been proven to be effective not only in schools and work, but when your trying to learn something new for yourself as well.

When you think on about practice and repetition a good example to help make this clear is to think about high school and test taking. We explain how when you're in high school you repeat information to yourself over and over because the teachers wanted to make sure that the information was going to stick in your head. We explained that same concept in this book and explain how it helps you to learn the information faster and make sure that it sticks in your head more quickly and more permanently. You want this information to stay in your head and you want to learn as much as you can while being able to use it to your advantage. We go over why this is so important in the book and how it's going to be able to help you achieve success in your life and in your career because this is vital information that you need to know.

Through this book you'll be able to understand the neurological responses in your brain and the skills and tips that we've been telling you are going to help you understand not only what skills you need but why you need them. You'll be able to understand why your body and your brain are acting the way that they are as well. When we do certain things are brain acts a certain way and that's why certain people respond to different skills and learning styles while others don't. As well as giving you basic information this book has also given you scientific information, facts and everything you need to know to make sure that you are able to progress further with yourself and further with your career. By utilizing the skills that you see in this book and by utilizing the tips that you find in this book you will be able to use generalism to your benefit and achieve success in your life.